MW01140520

A
HISTORY
OF MY
LIFE
FOR YOU

A HISTORY OF MY LIFE

FOR YOU

Bob Sasyniuk
and
Carol Campbell

iUniverse®

A HISTORY OF MY LIFE FOR YOU

Copyright © 2015 Bob Sasyniuk and Carol Campbell.

Illustrations by: Cameron Sasyniuk
Alexis Pasin

All rights reserved. No part of this book may be used or reproduced by any means, graphic, electronic, or mechanical, including photocopying, recording, taping or by any information storage retrieval system without the written permission of the publisher except in the case of brief quotations embodied in critical articles and reviews.

iUniverse books may be ordered through booksellers or by contacting:

iUniverse
1663 Liberty Drive
Bloomington, IN 47403
www.iuniverse.com
1-800-Authors (1-800-288-4677)

Because of the dynamic nature of the Internet, any web addresses or links contained in this book may have changed since publication and may no longer be valid. The views expressed in this work are solely those of the author and do not necessarily reflect the views of the publisher, and the publisher hereby disclaims any responsibility for them.

Any people depicted in stock imagery provided by Thinkstock are models, and such images are being used for illustrative purposes only. Certain stock imagery © Thinkstock.

ISBN: 978-1-4917-7520-2 (sc)
ISBN: 978-1-4917-7521-9 (hc)
ISBN: 978-1-4917-7522-6 (e)

Library of Congress Control Number: 2015913345

Print information available on the last page.

iUniverse rev. date: 11/24/2015

THIS BOOK IS FOR:

THIS BOOK IS FROM:

FAMILY HISTORY

Additional notes:

I WAS BORN:

MY PARENTS ARE:

MY GRANDPARENTS ARE:

MY SIBLINGS ARE:

MY
EARLY
LIFE

WHERE I GREW UP:

_____
_____
_____
_____
_____
_____
_____

ABOUT MY FAMILY:

_____
_____
_____
_____
_____
_____
_____

PETS:

_____
_____
_____
_____
_____
_____
_____
_____

MY EARLIEST CHILDHOOD MEMORY WAS:

MY FAVORITE CHILDHOOD MEMORY WAS:

Additional notes:

OTHER THINGS I REMEMBER ABOUT MY EARLY CHILDHOOD:

WHAT I WANTED TO BE WHEN I GREW UP:

Additional notes:

MY FIRST BEST FRIEND WAS:

_____

_____

_____

_____

_____

MY FIRST SCHOOL WAS:

_____

_____

_____

_____

_____

MY FAVORITE SUBJECT(S) WERE:

_____

_____

_____

_____

_____

MY FAVORITE TEACHER(S) WERE:

_____

_____

_____

_____

_____

_____

WHAT I WAS GOOD AT IN ELEMENTARY SCHOOL:

WHAT I WAS NOT GOOD AT IN ELEMENTARY SCHOOL:

Additional notes:

MY FRIENDS IN ELEMENTARY SCHOOL WERE:

SPORTS/HOBBIES/THINGS I LIKED TO DO:

MY TEEN YEARS

WHERE I LIVED:

MY FAMILY UPDATE:

PETS:

MY MIDDLE/HIGH SCHOOL/POST SECONDARY WAS:

MY FAVORITE TEACHER WAS:

Additional notes:

MY FAVORITE CLASS/SUBJECT WAS:

_____

_____

_____

_____

_____

_____

_____

MY LEAST FAVORITE CLASS/SUBJECT WAS:

_____

_____

_____

_____

_____

_____

_____

THE TYPE OF STUDENT I WAS:

_____

_____

_____

_____

_____

_____

_____

_____

Additional notes:

OTHER MIDDLE/HIGH SCHOOL/POST SECONDARY MEMORIES:

Additional notes:

MY FAVORITE TEEN MEMORY WAS:

MY WORST TEEN MEMORY WAS:

MY BEST FRIEND(S) WERE:

MY FIRST JOB(S) THAT I HAD:

SPORTS/HOBBIES/THINGS I LIKED TO DO:

Additional notes:

THINGS I WAS GOOD AT:

THINGS THAT I WAS NOT GOOD AT:

GOOD/BAD HABITS THAT I HAD:

MY IDOL(S) GROWING UP WERE:

Additional notes:

PERSON(S) THAT HAD THE MOST EFFECT ON MY LIFE:

MY FIRST CAR WAS:

MY FIRST RELATIONSHIP WAS WITH:

MY FAVORITE T.V. SHOW WAS:

MY FAVORITE MOVIE WAS:

MY FAVORITE ACTOR/ACTRESS WAS:

MY FAVORITE MUSIC WAS:

MY FAVORITE BAND WAS:

Additional notes:

MY FAVORITE BOOK WAS:

MY FAVORITE SPORTS/SPORTS TEAM/PLAYER WAS:

THE KIND OF CLOTHES THAT I WORE WERE:

Additional notes:

MY FAVORITE FOOD/RESTAURANT WAS:

MY FAVORITE TRIP/VACATION WAS:

IMPORTANT OR OTHER EVENTS OF/DURING MY TEEN YEARS:

EARLY ADULT YEARS

Additional notes:

WHERE I LIVED:

MY FAMILY UPDATE:

PETS:

JOBS THAT I HAD:

MY FAVORITE MEMORY WAS:

MY WORST MEMORY WAS:

Additional notes:

MY BEST FRIEND/FRIENDS WERE:

RELATIONSHIPS:

Additional notes:

SPORTS/HOBBIES/THINGS I LIKED TO DO:

THINGS THAT I WAS GOOD AT:

Additional notes:

THINGS THAT I WAS NOT GOOD AT:

GOOD/BAD HABITS THAT I HAD:

Additional notes:

MY CAR(S) WERE:

_____

_____

_____

_____

_____

_____

_____

MY FAVORITE T.V. SHOW WAS:

_____

_____

_____

_____

_____

_____

_____

MY FAVORITE MOVIE WAS:

_____

_____

_____

_____

_____

_____

_____

_____

MY FAVORITE ACTOR/ACTRESS WAS:

MY FAVORITE MUSIC WAS:

MY FAVORITE BAND WAS:

Additional notes:

MY FAVORITE BOOK WAS:

MY FAVORITE SPORTS/SPORTS TEAM/PLAYER WAS:

THE KIND OF CLOTHES THAT I WORE/MY STYLE WAS:

Additional notes:

MY FAVORITE FOOD WAS:

MY FAVORITE VACATION WAS:

OTHER PLACES THAT I TRAVELLED OR VISITED:

IMPORTANT OR OTHER EVENTS OF/DURING MY EARLY ADULTHOOD:

THE
REST

WHERE I LIVE:

MY FAMILY UPDATE:

PETS:

MY FAVORITE COLOR IS:

MY FAVORITE SMELL IS:

MY FAVORITE THING TO DO/THINGS THAT MAKE
ME HAPPY ARE:

Additional notes:

MY LEAST FAVORITE THING TO DO/THINGS THAT
MAKE ME SAD ARE:

MY FAVORITE SEASON/TIME OF THE YEAR IS:

MY FAVORITE PART OF THE DAY IS:

MY FAVORITE DECADE WAS/IS:

THE YEAR OF THE BEST BIRTHDAY I EVER HAD:

THE MOST FAVORITE GIFT I GAVE/RECEIVED:

Additional notes:

THE FAVORITE ITEM NOBODY KNOWS I OWN:

MUSIC THAT I LISTEN TO NOW (BAND/BANDS/ ARTISTS):

FAVORITE T.V. SHOW(S):

FAVORITE MOVIE(S):

FAVORITE BOOK(S):

FAVORITE FOOD/RESTAURANT:

FAVORITE COLD/HOT DRINK:

Additional notes:

FAVORITE VACATION SPOT(S):

_____

_____

_____

_____

_____

_____

FAVORITE SPORTING ACTIVITIES/HOBBIES/ INTERESTS:

_____

_____

_____

_____

_____

_____

_____

THINGS THAT FRIGHTEN ME:

_____

_____

_____

_____

_____

_____

_____

Additional notes:

SCARIEST THING THAT I EVER DID/OR HAPPENED TO ME:

THE BEST THING THAT EVER HAPPENED TO/FOR ME:

THE THING/THINGS THAT I AM MOST PROUD OF:

I DREAMT OF BEING:

Additional notes:

THING OR THINGS THAT I WISH I HAD DONE DIFFERENTLY IN MY LIFE:

Additional notes:

THINGS THAT I WISH I WOULD HAVE DONE/MY BUCKET LIST:

THE KIND OF PERSON THAT I FEEL THAT I AM:

AWARDS AND ACCOMPLISHMENTS:

BELIEFS THAT I HAVE:

Additional notes:

MY FAVORITE HOLIDAY TIME OF THE YEAR:

PEOPLE THAT ARE MY FRIENDS:

Additional notes:

THE BEST ADVICE I'VE EVER BEEN GIVEN:

THE BEST ADVICE I'VE EVER GIVEN:

MESSAGES TO YOU

This page dedicated for photos, documents, etc.

CPSIA information can be obtained at www.ICGtesting.com
Printed in the USA
LVOW12*2358290116

472009LV00001B/8/P